Words

Illustrator
Sonia Canals

Consultants
Penny Coltman
and Jayne Greenwood

in the house

lamp

table

pillow

toys

bed

cat

picture

curtains

window

television

book

chair

rug

dinnertime

bedtime

night

days of the week

Monday

Tuesday

Wednesday

Thursday

Friday

Saturday

Sunday

Monday
Tuesday
Wednesday
Thursday
Friday
Saturday
Sunday

seasons

spring

summer

vehicles

plane

lorry

bike

car

train

tractor

boat

motorbike

people who help us

nurse

doctor

police

skipping

hide and seek

climb

jump

crawl

positional words

in

out

through

next to

between

over

on

under

body parts

eyes

fingers

hand

head

nose

ears

mouth

arm

elbow

chest

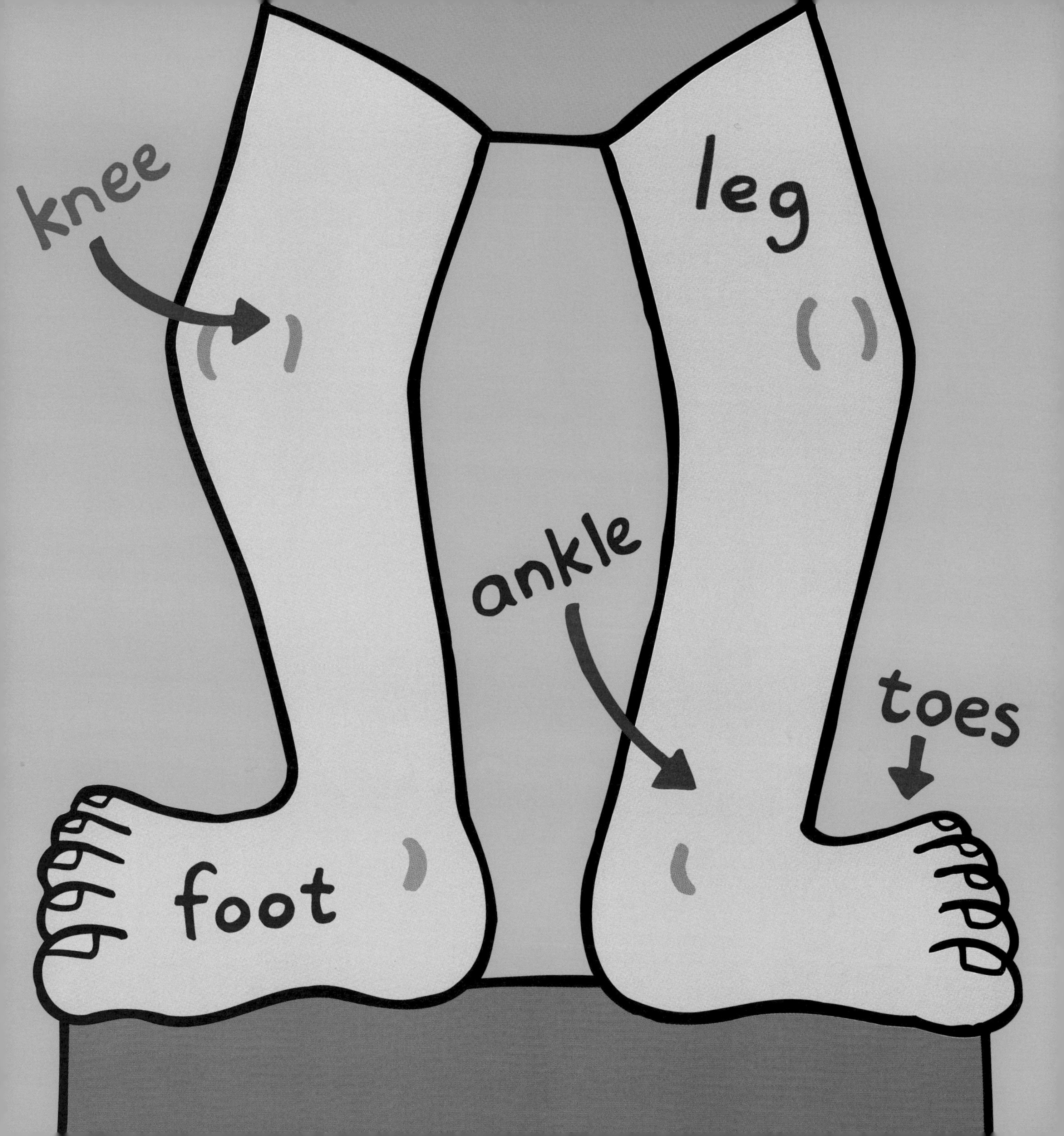
knee
leg
ankle
toes
foot

dress

coat

jeans

skirt

vest

food

bread

apple

cucumber

sandwich

baked beans

pizza

crisps

orange

chocolate

chips

grapes

pets

parrot

dog

mouse

hamster

elephant

crocodile

giraffe

Match the things that go together.

sock

saucer

ball

fork

fish

paper

bye bye!

..........Notes for Parents

Using This Book

Explanation

This book will help you to introduce your child to the idea of words and their meanings.

Sharing this book should be seen as fun. Choose a time when both you and your child feel relaxed and comfortable.

Remember that little and often is the best recipe for success. Give plenty of praise and encouragement and remember that the golden rule is to stop when it becomes clear that your child has 'had enough'.

With your child

- Look at the cover of the book together. Introduce words such as 'cover', 'page' and 'title'.
- Talk together about the pictures on the cover.
- Look together at the words on the cover of the book. Explain that some of the words tell the reader who wrote the book or drew the pictures.
- As you look through the pages chat about the pictures you see, recognising familiar objects and helping your child to learn about some new ones. Underneath each picture is a word. Point these out to your child, and explain that these letters say the name of the object.

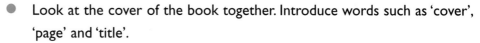
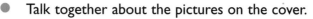
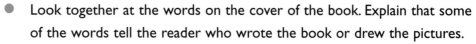

n
o
t
e
s

Introducing Words

notes

Explanation

All the words in this book involve ideas and situations which will be familiar to your young child.

As you read through the book together your child will soon understand that every object in the book has an accompanying word. Older children will begin to be able to recognise individual words.

Some of the longer words, such as 'elephant', are often easier for children to recognise than short words such as 'the'. This is because the word has a distinctive shape.

With your child

- Look together at the first page in the book. Encourage your child to talk about what they can see. Draw attention to the words by each picture and read them to your child.

- All the objects on this page are household items. Encourage your child to make links between the pictures on the page and the actual objects.

- Talk together about other objects which might have been included on this page.

........Notes for Parents

Making Connections

Explanation

Many of the words in this book are easy for
children to understand through looking at the pictures
and talking about them.

Each double page spread contains words and pictures which belong to
a particular theme.

Wherever possible use real objects to show your child examples of the
words on the pages.

Help your child to think of their own examples to add to each theme from
his/her own everyday experiences.

With your child

- Use a toy and a small box to help your child to understand position
  words such as 'in', 'on', 'inside', 'next to' and 'under'. Hide the toy in the
  room and use these words as you help your child to look for it.

- Match the body part words to the parts of a teddy.
- Copy some of the words onto cards. Encourage your child to match them to
  words on the page and then to use the cards to label objects in the home.

Games to Play

Explanation

Playing games will help your child to understand more about the meanings and sounds of words.

Your child will benefit from trying a variety of games. It is known that learning through play is one of the best ways of developing skills.

As children become more confident, they enjoy taking turns in both asking and answering questions.

With your child

- Play spotting games with your child using the pages in the book:
  - ◆ Can you find something with lots of wheels, which goes very fast?
  - ◆ Can you find a picture of a person who might mend a broken down car?
- Encourage your child to look at one of the double page spreads very carefully. Now cover one of the pictures with your hand. Challenge your child to identify the 'missing' picture, giving clues to help:
  'The animal which is covered up is small and it lives in water.'
- Older children will enjoy playing a game of 'I Spy' using a double page spread. This will also help them to practise listening to and recognising the sounds at the beginnings of words.

.........Notes for Parents

Words Around Us

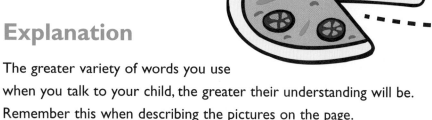

Explanation

The greater variety of words you use
when you talk to your child, the greater their understanding will be.
Remember this when describing the pictures on the page.

Children are surrounded by words and it is helpful to explain to children
that these words have meaning and give information.

With your child

Here are some examples of the types of everyday situations in which
children come across words.

- Point out words in the supermarket: on packages, on your shopping list,
  or hanging on large notices above the aisles.
- Look at the words you see on the roads and streets: on road signs,
  above shops or on information signs.
- Point out words in advertisements on the television or in newspapers
  and magazines.
- Help your child to see that written words give
  information by showing how you use instruction
  books, recipe books, game rules or travel guides.

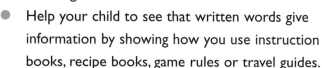

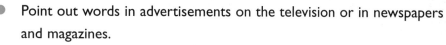

Songs and Rhymes

Explanation

Songs and rhymes can be used to encourage children to enjoy playing with words, to help them learn new words and to help them understand words.

Nonsense songs help children to use a variety of sounds with confidence.

Rhymes are known to be very important in helping children learn to read.

With your child

- Sing some well-known songs with nonsense words. Good examples include:
  - ◆ Nick Nack Paddywack   ◆ Diddle Diddle Dumpling.
- Take a well-known word and play at adding new initial letters to make rhyming strings of words, for example: fairy, hairy, scary, Mary.
- Children particularly enjoy playing this using their names as starting points. The words made do not need to make sense! For example: Lizzy, fizzy, bizzy, dizzy, wizzy.
- Some of the old traditional nursery rhymes introduce quite complicated language:
  - ◆ Sing a Song of Sixpence   ◆ Little Miss Muffet.
- Look through the pictures in the book and think of songs to associate with them:
  - ◆ Pussy Cat, Pussy Cat   ◆ Twinkle Twinkle Little Star.

.... Notes for Parents

Putting Words Together

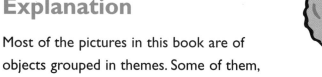

Explanation

Most of the pictures in this book are of objects grouped in themes. Some of them, however, can be used together as children begin to make connections.

It is also helpful to encourage children to add describing words, or even to begin to make up their own sentences about the objects in the book.

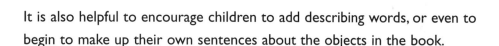

With your child

- Make some colour word labels by writing colour words next to patches of colour on some small cards. Show your child how to place the label next to appropriate pictures. A label with the word 'yellow', for example, could be placed next to a yellow hat, a yellow moon or a yellow sun.
- Match the body-part words with pictures from one of the 'animals' pages to make phrases such as 'an elephant's knee' or 'a rabbit's nose'.
- Use the position words to describe other objects in the book:
  - ◆ The boy is on the sledge.
  - ◆ The fish is in the bowl.
  - ◆ The girl is hiding behind her hands.

 Notes for Parents

Using the Matching Pairs Page

Explanation

This page introduces some examples of words which go together. Some of the words can be found on other pages in the book, and others are new.

As you talk about the pictures encourage your child to suggest words to describe them.

The idea of the puzzle is to encourage your child to identify the pairs of objects.

With your child

Talk about the pictures on the double page spread.

- Encourage your child to choose one of the pictures and to say what it is.
- Help your child to then look at the remaining pictures and to decide which one goes with the chosen object – for example, a foot goes with a sock.
- Talk about why the objects form a pair. What do they have in common?
- Make your own 'object matching game', using objects from around the house. Examples might include:
  - a brush and a comb
  - a bowl and a spoon
  - a tooth brush and a tube of toothpaste.